READ ABOUT

Hurricanes

Sally Morgan

COPPER BEECH BOOKS
BROOKFIELD • CONNECTICUT

Contents

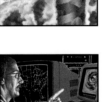

© Aladdin Books Ltd 2000

Designed and produced by
Aladdin Books Ltd
28 Percy Street
London W1P 0LD

First published in
the United States in 2000 by
Copper Beech Books,
an imprint of
The Millbrook Press
2 Old New Milford Road
Brookfield, Connecticut 06804

ISBN 0 7613 1174 2
Cataloging-in-Publication data is on file
at the Library of Congress.

Printed in Belgium

All rights reserved

Editor
Jim Pipe

Science Consultant
Julian Heming, Meteorological Office

Series Literacy Consultant
Wendy Cobb

Design
Flick Killerby Book Design and Graphics

Picture Research
Brooks Krikler Research

What is a Hurricane?

Hurricanes are violent storms that happen in tropical (warm) parts of the world. They are one of the most powerful, scary forces in nature. Nothing can be done to stop them.

These big storms can be 1,000 miles wide. They bring very large rain clouds and very fast winds.

When a hurricane moves over the land, the strong winds smash through towns and villages. They knock houses and trees flat.

You can see the hurricane winds blowing the leaves.

What do you think has happened here? The answer is on page 32.

The winds toss cars into the air, like you would throw a toy. Rivers of water run down from the hills. They wash away trees, roads, and bridges.

When the storm passes, some towns are completely destroyed. There is no water, no fresh food, and no electricity. Sometimes, thousands of people are killed and many more are left without homes.

Read on to find out about these terrible storms. Learn why they start, where they happen, and how people can prepare for them.

Where in the World?

Hurricanes • Cyclones • Typhoons

Big tropical storms are found near the equator (an imaginary line half way between the North and South poles). They happen over seas where the water is very warm (see map on page 6).

These violent storms have different names in different parts of the world. They are called hurricanes in the Caribbean Sea, in the southern U.S., and in Central America.

A hurricane swept these ships ashore.

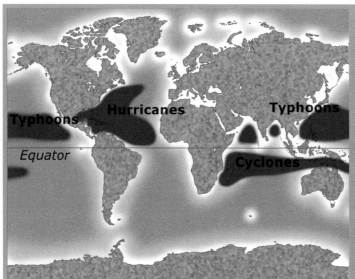

Typhoons, cyclones, and hurricanes happen near the equator – a line that marks half way between the North and South poles.

Hurricanes in the China Sea and the northern Pacific Ocean are called typhoons. Typhoons happen in southern China, the Philippines, and Japan. Typhoon means "big wind" in Chinese.

Cyclones are the hurricanes of the Indian Ocean. Cyclones happen in the northern part of Australia, Indonesia, India, and Bangladesh.

In this book, we call all of these storms hurricanes. But a cyclone or a typhoon is exactly the same as a hurricane.

A Hurricane Begins

All tropical storms start over warm water (like the water in the picture). But the water must be very warm before a hurricane will happen.

The warm water heats the air above it. It also makes the air steamy, as the air is mixed with water gas rising from the sea.

The hot, wet air creates storms. In summer, when the water is warmest, these storms can turn into a hurricane. This is how it happens...

When air is warmed up, it spreads out, or expands. As it expands, the air gets lighter. This makes it rise into the sky.

You can see how warm air rises at home. Put your hand above a hot radiator. You will be able to feel the warm air rising from the top of the radiator.

Near the floor you may be able to feel the cold air moving toward the radiator to replace the warm air. The same thing causes the winds of a hurricane, but on a much bigger scale.

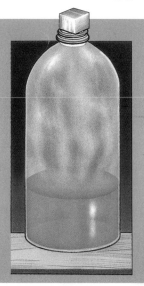

Make your own tiny rain cloud like this...
1 Fill a large plastic bottle with hot water.
2 Pour out two thirds of the water.

3 Place an ice cube on top of the bottle.
4 The hot water gas forms a misty cloud when it meets the cold ice cube.

A current of warm air rises into the sky. Then cooler air moves in from the area around it to replace it. This is the movement we call wind.

But what about the rain? Well, the warm air is also wet. As it rises, it gets cooler. The water gas in the air changes back into liquid water. These droplets form rain clouds.

As more gas turns into droplets, the clouds grow bigger and bigger. Warm air continues to rise from the ocean, and more cool air is pulled into the storm. The winds get stronger.

The water droplets in rain clouds make them look dark.

How a Hurricane Begins

1 Warm air rises from the ocean.

2 Cold air rushes in to replace it. This creates wind.

3 The spinning earth makes the winds spin around and around.

The winds are also pulled by the earth. As our planet spins around and around, it makes winds near the equator spin around, too.

The winds move in a spiral and make the clouds spin. When this happens, a group of storm clouds turn into a spinning hurricane!

Inside a Hurricane

The Eye of a Storm • How Big Is a Hurricane?

Imagine you are standing right in front of a hurricane. Look up and all you can see is a block of storm clouds reaching into the sky.

It's a huge wall of clouds. The clouds are full of water. This makes them look dark and scary. Strong winds blow around the storm clouds. They are so strong you can hardly stand up.

The black clouds of an approaching hurricane.

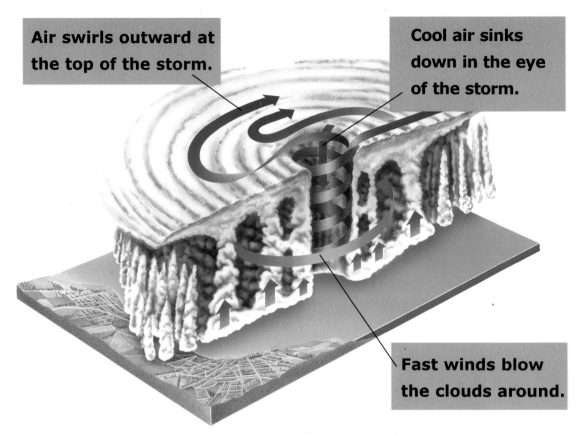

Air swirls outward at the top of the storm.

Cool air sinks down in the eye of the storm.

Fast winds blow the clouds around.

Now imagine you can walk through the clouds. The sky gets darker as you walk forward.

Once you are on the other side of the wall of clouds, you find yourself in the middle of the storm.

You can see clouds all around you, but there are no clouds in the sky right above you. The sky is clear and it's sunny. The winds have dropped, too, and it's very calm.

This is the central area which is called the eye of the storm. Here, cool air is sinking down. It's a bit like a donut — the wall of clouds form a ring with none in the middle.

If you keep on walking, you pass through to the other side of the storm. This time the winds are blowing in the opposite direction.

The eye of a hurricane seen from space

Once the big blocks of clouds have formed, the hurricane starts to move across the ocean.

As long as it stays over warm water, damp air is always rising from the ocean. This damp air gives the hurricane its energy. Over a few hours, the winds blow faster and faster.

The difference between a normal storm and a hurricane is the speed of the wind.

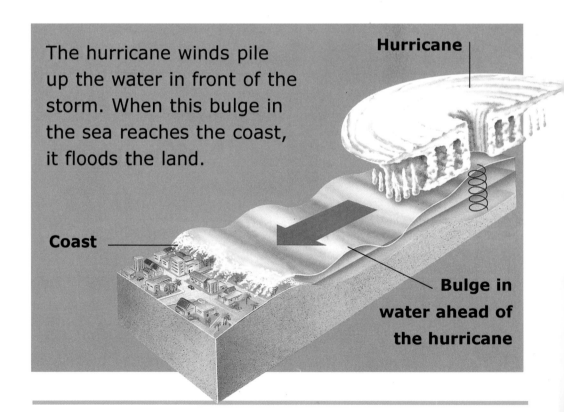

The hurricane winds pile up the water in front of the storm. When this bulge in the sea reaches the coast, it floods the land.

Hurricane

Coast

Bulge in water ahead of the hurricane

Once the wind speeds reach about 75 miles per hour, a storm can be called a hurricane. The faster the winds are in a hurricane, the more powerful the hurricane is.

Scientists group hurricanes according to their wind speed. The strongest hurricanes have speeds of over 155 miles per hour. They are called Category 5 hurricanes and they cause the most damage.

Do you think it is safe to walk in a hurricane? Answer on page 32.

Luckily, there are very few Category 5 hurricanes. Only two Category 5 hurricanes have hit the United States in the last 100 years.

Hurricanes are very large. Most are about 300 miles wide. Some are 1,000 miles across. But a bigger hurricane is not always more powerful.

Hurricanes can be seen clearly by satellites – spacecraft that watch the earth from space.

HURRICANE STRENGTHS

Type		Windspeed	Damage	Example (year)
Storm		31-72 mph	little	Aren't named
Category	1	73-94 mph	not much	Florence 1988

Type		Windspeed	Damage	Example (year)
Category	2	95-108 mph	quite a bit	Earl 1998
Category	3	109-128 mph	bad	Fran 1996

Type		Windspeed	Damage	Example (year)
Category	4	129-154 mph	very bad	Andrew 1988
Category	5	over 155 mph	terrible	Mitch 1988

Early Warnings

Hurricanes begin over the ocean, far away from towns and cities. So getting information about hurricanes needs special equipment.

People who study the weather are called meteorologists (say "meaty-your-all-oh-jists"). They follow storms using pictures of the earth. Satellites take these pictures from space.

The pictures are taken over many hours. They show the direction and speed of the storm.

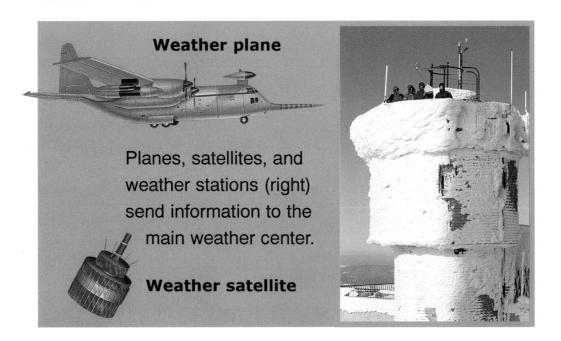

Weather plane

Planes, satellites, and weather stations (right) send information to the main weather center.

Weather satellite

Ships and planes near the hurricane collect information on their instruments. Some planes fly right into the eye of the hurricane to measure the speed of the wind.

Ships measure the heat of the sea around the storm. If the hurricane is moving toward warmer water, it will often get stronger.

Once a hurricane has been spotted, it is given a name. Some names are just letters and numbers, others are people's names.

Satellite pictures can show how fast a hurricane is moving.

In the Atlantic, the first hurricane of the year is given a name beginning with A. The next hurricane will begin with B and so on.

For example, in 1999 the first hurricane was called Arlene. The next one was called Bret.

It is important that people who live in the path of a hurricane get as much warning as possible. People need time to prepare for the hurricane.

They may have to move animals in from the fields and cover up their windows. People may have to move out of the area.

In some areas, there are shelters for people. These can stand up to the strong winds.

A police officer tells a driver to get out of the storm.

The Hurricane Hits

Driving Rain • Strong Winds • Giant Waves

The first sign that the hurricane is getting close is the wind. It gets stronger and rain starts to fall.

The leaves blow about in the wind and litter is picked up from the ground. Waves along the coast get higher.

The winds continue to pick up speed. Whole trees are bent right over by the wind. Strong winds and rain lash against windows.

The wind gets stronger still. The sky grows dark as the large black storm clouds pass above. Buckets of rain fall to the ground.

Being in a hurricane is very scary.

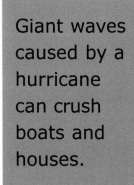

Giant waves caused by a hurricane can crush boats and houses.

Violent winds overturn cars and blow the roofs off buildings. Weak houses are blown over. The winds pull down electric cables and cut off the power.

Huge waves batter the coast and flood the flat land near the sea. The rain water runs off the high ground into streams and rivers.

The rivers rise and flood their banks. The flood waters sweep down to the coast, carrying with them cars, bikes, and lots of other objects.

Anyone falling into the water is quickly washed away. The water also washes away the bottom parts of buildings and bridges and makes them collapse.

This first part of the hurricane may last six or more hours. Then, all of a sudden, the winds die down and the rain stops.

But the hurricane is not over yet. Everything is calm because the eye of the storm passes over.

The storm goes quiet.

Within an hour or so, the violent wind and rain returns. This time, the wind is blowing in the opposite direction.

Any buildings that survived the first time around may collapse when the winds return.

The hurricane winds blow over the surface of the water. They whip up extra-high waves that crash into the coast.

Hurricanes create enormous waves at sea. These sank many wooden sailing ships in the past.

Imagine blowing over the surface of the water in a bath. You create a few ripples. If you blow really hard, you can make small waves.

This is what happens out at sea. The waves rush inland, causing a flood.

Waves crash into the coast.

A Dying Storm

A hurricane gets its energy from the warm sea. But as soon as it moves over land, it loses this energy. The air over the land is drier and there is less warm and wet air rising up into the sky. So the winds die down.

Now people have to clear up the mess. There is junk and water everywhere.

Hurricane winds have flipped this plane over.

The electricity and the water may be cut off for many days. It will take engineers a long time to repair all the broken cables and pipes.

The hurricane becomes just a storm. Even so, it can still damage trees and power lines, and plenty of rain still falls.

Villages and towns may be cut off by blocked roads. Food may be in short supply. But soon help arrives and the repairs can get started.

Find Out More

PICTURE QUIZ

Can you think of five things that happen in a hurricane? Look at the pictures below for some clues. They can all be found in this book. The answers are on page 32.

UNUSUAL WORDS

Here we explain some words you may have read in this book.

Air current The movement of air.

Cyclone The name for a hurricane that happens near India, Indonesia, and northern Australia.

Equator The imaginary line that runs around the middle of the earth.

Evacuation When people move away from a danger area to a safe place.

Eye The central calm area of a hurricane.

Instrument A machine that measures things or does a task.

Meteorologist (meaty-your-all-oh-jist) A scientist who studies the weather.

Pressure Another word for force.

Satellite An instrument that floats around the earth in space and sends back information.

Satellite

Shelter A place built to keep people safe.

Storm A period of bad weather with heavy rain and strong winds.

Tropical Something found near to the equator, such as a tropical island or a tropical storm.

Typhoon The name for a hurricane in south China, Japan, and the northern Pacific Ocean.

Hurricane Myths

The word hurricane comes from "Huracan," the name of the West Indian god of storms. In Japan, people believed that the god Raijin caused big storms (left). The sound of thunder was Raijin beating on his drums.

SOME BIG HURRICANES

Cyclones in Asia

Cyclones cause a lot of damage in southern Asia (right). In 1971, the floods caused by a cyclone killed more than half a million people in Bangladesh.

Hurricanes in the Caribbean

In 1988, Hurricane Gilbert hit Mexico and the West Indies. It was the most powerful hurricane in the last 200 years, and it killed 300 people.

Cyclones in Australia

Cyclone Tracey struck Darwin in northern Australia in 1974. It destroyed 90 percent of the buildings in the city.

Index

ANSWERS TO PICTURE QUESTIONS

Page 4 The hurricane rains have caused a river to flood. The people have been forced to leave their home.

Page 15 Fast hurricane winds can easily knock you over. So it's very dangerous to go out in them.

Page 30 Five things that happen in a hurricane are: **1** Rains cause flooding. **2** Big waves batter the coast. **3** Strong winds knock trees and houses flat. **4** Electric power lines are cut. **5** Rivers wash away houses and bridges.

Illustrators: Stephen Sweet – SGA, Ian Thompson, Pete Roberts – Allied Artists, Guy Smith
Photocredits: *Abbreviations: t-top, m-middle, b-bottom, r-right, l-left, c-center.* Cover and Pages 13, 15, 17t & m & 24 – Oxford Scientific Films; 1, 3, 4, 16, 17b, 19, 20, 25, 27, 28 & 31 all – Rex Features; 5, 11, 21, 22, 23 & 29 – Frank Spooner Pictures.